THIS

SHERIFF GRADY JUDD

COLORING BOOK

BELONGS TO:

_ _ _ _ _ _ _ _ _ _ _ _ _ _

D. O. G. PUBLISHING

Copyright © 2022 by Dale O. Garrett and D.O.G. Publishing
All rights reserved. No portion of this book may be reproduced in any form without
The express written consent of the publisher, except as permitted by U.S. copyright laws.
PROUDLY PRINTED AND MAUFACTURED IN THE
UNITED STATES OF AMERICA

SHERIFF

SERVICE • EXCELLENCE
SERVICE
INTEGRITY

POLK COUNTY

I DO A HAPPY DANCE EVERY TIME WE GET ONE OF THESE BAD GUYS OFF THE STREET!

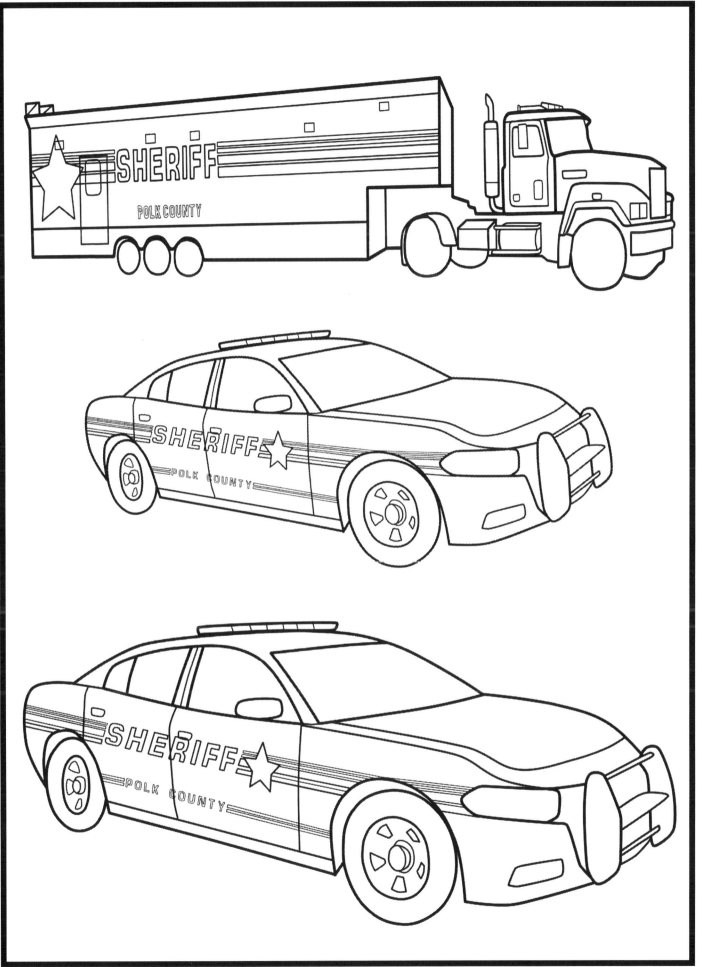

THIS BAD GUY ONLY HAS 3 BRAIN CELLS... AND 2 OF THEM AIN'T WORKIN'!

JUST CHILL OUT.
DRINK A 7-UP.
EAT A MOON PIE...

IF SHERIFF JUDD IS ON VACATION, MAYBE ONE OF THE SHERIFF'S K-9 DEPUTIES CAN FILL IN DURING PRESS CONFERENCES...

ARE YA KIDDIN' ME!?
C'MON MAN!

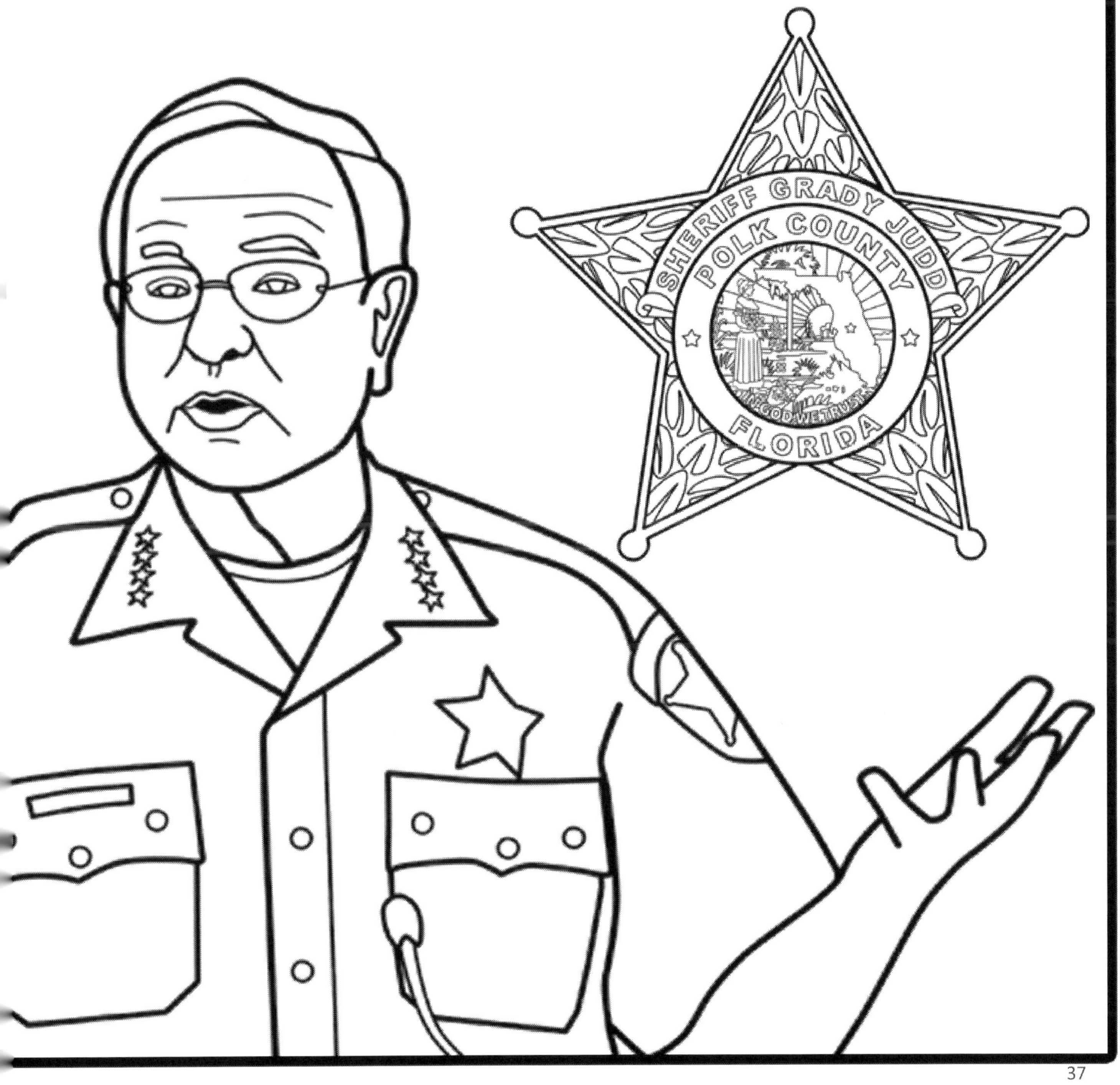

SHERIFF JUDD PROTECTS THE CHILDREN OF POLK COUNTY!

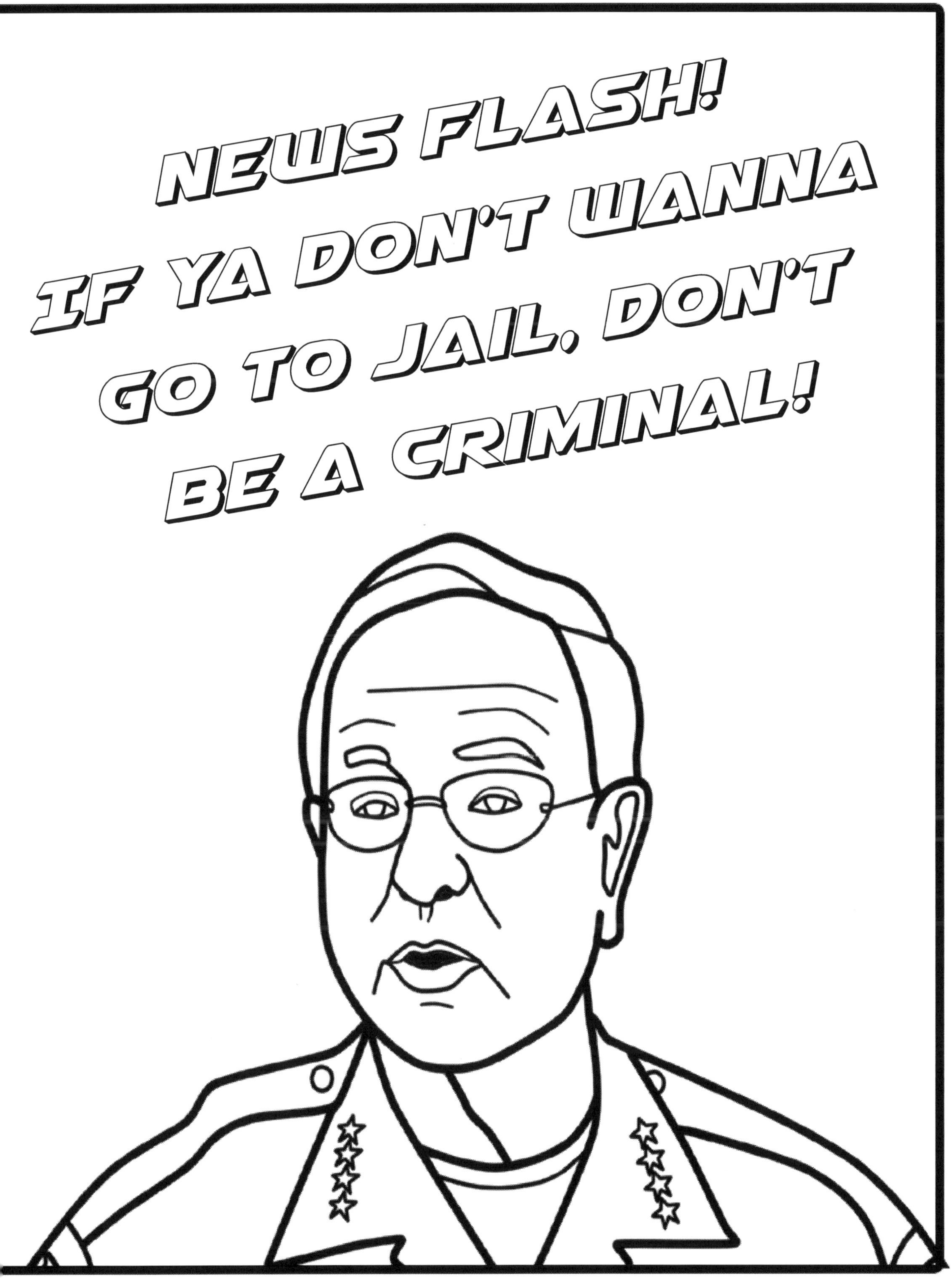
NEWS FLASH!
IF YA DON'T WANNA
GO TO JAIL, DON'T
BE A CRIMINAL!

IF YOU BUY JEWELRY WITH YOUR DRUG MONEY, WE WILL PUT YOU IN JAIL AND TAKE YOUR BLING!

I HAVE A MESSAGE FOR CRIMINALS... WE HAVE A ROOM FOR YOU IN THE POLK COUNTY JAIL!

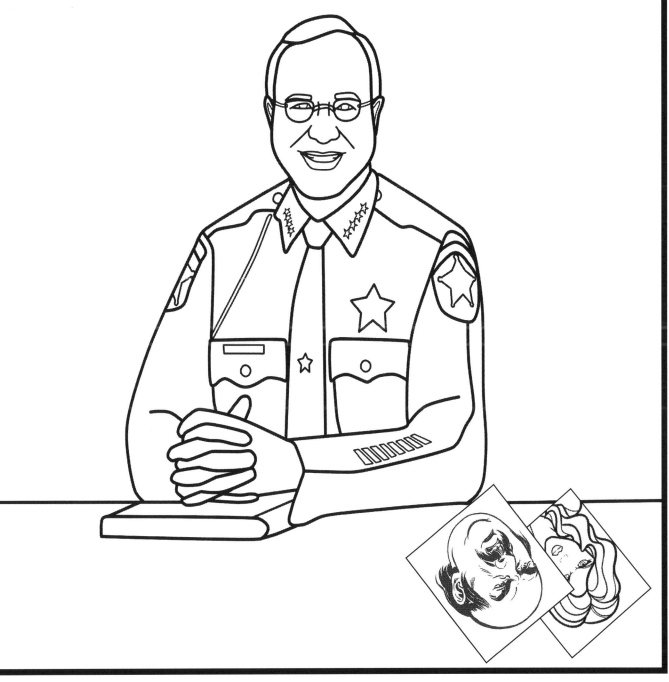

SHERIFF JUDD LOVES SHOOTING NATURE PHOTOS.
AND WHEN HE SHOOTS THEM, HE SHOOTS THEM A LOT!

SHERIFF JUDD LOVES POLK COUNTY AND POLK COUNTY LOVES SHERIFF JUDD!

For more books by this author, scan the below
QR code with your mobile phone or, visit:
www.Amazon.com/Author/DaleOGarrett

Made in United States
Orlando, FL
18 December 2024

56193086R00028

ISBN 9798840360668

sellbackyourBook

The Big Volleyball Coloring Book

A Volleyball Coloring Book For Teens and Adults

2nd Edition!

40 Designs!

By Debbie Russell